Wild Divinity

First edition, June 2020
Copyright © 2020 Lily Grace

Published by Penciled In
5319 Barrenda Avenue
Atascadero, CA 93422
penciledin.com

ISBN-13:   978-1-939502-40-7

Book and Cover Design
  by Benjamin Daniel Lawless

Cover photo
  Angel Dreams by Kamil Vojnar

Text is set in
  Arno Pro, Neutra Text

Wild Divinity

POEMS BY LILY GRACE

CONTENTS

For My Beloved
Max

Come celebrate with me,
that everyday something has
tried to kill me and has failed.
— Lucille Clifton, from the *Book of Light*

For every poet, it is always morning
in the world. Elemental awe is our early
beginning, because the fate of poetry,
is to fall in love with the world, in spite of history.
— Derek Walcott, Nobel Prize acceptance speech

You wouldn't believe what once or
twice I have seen. I'll just
     tell you this:
only if there are angels in your head will you
     ever, possibly, see one.
— Mary Oliver, from *Felicity*

Wild Divinity

Musical Stars

Rain and footprints
press the maples
into the wet pavement,
glittering gold, red, and yellow,
crinkled leaves fanning out, aflame
like fallen autumnal stars.

Walking this well-worn trail
alone once again,
years later, I remember
your shiny, silver toy jet,
somersaulting out of the sky
and crashing at my feet.

On that hot July evening
when fireflies flickered
through the trees,
 like orange neon stars,
all the earth's music stopped.
You said, *You are my roll,*
even at 20, intuiting
the dicey game of love.

Women, Preserving

Wu Wei: Chinese Taoist philosophy, based on the belief conserving energy creates internal balance and harmony.

Ooo, la la la
Ooooo weeeeee,
Laura Nyro's
sixties doo-wop
street music,
ignited our teen years
gave us language
for land mines tripping, our
bleeding bodies'
hormone-torment, & rapture swings,
played out on a losing war.

Your voice, Nyro, reached
down into our collective-deep,
reflected back our volatile emotions,
love and loss,
> *where we goin'*
> *to be so willin'*
> *for the killin'."*

Vietnam's father there,
brother, boyfriends dying
jungle fighting across the world.

The boys, scared, buried
themselves inside us...
into each white lily's slumber,
petals opening to their tongues.

Meeting Jack Tanner
in his father's stolen car,
radio rockin
turned on
in hot night's hood

super ride inside my love thing
would you love to love me baby.

the moon reflecting back in
our faces, & the moon
between my legs.

Behind locked bedroom doors.
Jorie turned me on to your voice
Nyro, and to my clitoris, hiding
pulsating pink sea anemone.

You belted out lyrics
simmering in every sentient
young woman's wounded
heart, giving us courage
to shout our communal cry:

don't try to put me in a box.
I am too long, wide and deep
to be contained.
>   *don't mess with me.*
>   *don't look at me like Freud,*
>   *this could create a void.*

In *"Woman of the World"*
your voice begins in a slow burn
erupting into SOS flares,
shooting heavenward –

I'm movin' up in school,
where I've learned to play it cool.
I was a foolish girl,
but now I'm a woman
of the world."

Again your voice
fills my kitchen while I chop onions
for a winter stew, remember
our serpentine pilgrimage,
swooning swans, our young
want & wasting
becoming
self-attending, wise women
having learned
to preserve our wu wei.

Milkshake Day

Beshert: Yiddish word, denoting a gift bearing the fingerprint of divine providence, commonly used in reference to a life partner, but not exclusively.
Nephesh: Hebrew word meaning: appetite, lust, passion.

Pop would call this
a beshert day, a milkshake day,
misty milky opaque skies,
filled with honking geese,
aching for home,
snow soon to fall,
burying all wishes,
under the white of waiting.

It is a day to revel in lostness
splurging on cream and calories,
the finest quality chocolate.

I am his granddaughter, after all
today we will share our *nephesh*
for this simple sacramental luxury
sliding down the throat,
like the tongue of God
erasing all betrayals,
that once ravaged the soul.

Locked in the divine embrace
this lush, silky rich ratio
of ice cream to milk and syrup,
floating ice cream clouds
blended just enough
to create amniotic bliss,
a blessed balm
for the savage heart.

Winter Fishpond

**What happens to the ducks at Central Park lagoon
in the winter?**
— JD Salinger, *Catcher In the Rye*

My father held my small hand as we circled
the pond in the cemetery, the only water
in our asphalt-and-steel-mill town.
Teenage girls slipped out to the moonlit
mortuary at night for their first kiss
under a tiara of stars.
It was a dreamy place my father chose
to take me one last time,
before he vanished from my world,
leaving love and longing eternally
coupled inside my pink heart.

We stopped along the frosted edge
of the fishpond, our eyes fastened
on the blurry orange smears below, still
as the granite gravestones surrounding them
until after the spring thaw when the goldfish
would magically resurrect.

For years I have wondered where they went
when the waters turned icy and indifferent.
Perhaps to some interior cathedral
buried in a wintry silence – suspended, frozen,
learning year after year, how to disappear.

Wolf's Neck, Maine

**"It wasn't the airplanes;
it was beauty killed the beast,"**
— Carl Denham, *King Kong*

The dog and I walk to the top
of the hill through a thicket
of deep woods canopied
with lacy moss.
Below, the slate sea
crashes into the rocks.
Windblown leaves swirl
gold, red, and orange flames,
through autumnal apple crisp air.
Heart-stopping beauty
caused a deadly collision
along the two-lane country road.
It was too dangerous to drive that day.
The eye gravitating
toward the glowing trees,
as if they were lit from within.
The mind on fire with possibility.

Blindfolded

Happy families are all alike; every unhappy family is unhappy in its own way.
— Leo Tolstoy, *Anna Karenina*

Missing puzzle pieces
from my dead marriage
appear unbidden like lost
limbs or forgotten prodigals:

The birthday you blindfolded me
guiding me into your shiny, black F-150,
and swept me away to a seaside inn;

The gift lying on the white
poplin bedspread, *Love Poems From God.*
The dazzling inscription: *To the love of my life.*

The morning you traced the outline
of my back with your index finger,
and said a blind man should paint
the canvas of my back,
to know perfection.

My first meeting with your mother
at the state asylum,
recovering from electric shock.
She stared into space like a disoriented astronaut.

The romance of your unhappy family
a magnetic pull too powerful
for a young poet.

If I could grab that girl,
I'd tell her:
It's not too late.
Save yourself, walk away.
In the end, there will be a train,
and you will think
the only cure for your homeless heart,
raw as an unshelled clam,
will be under that black, barreling,
  locomotive steaming through town.

Instead, jumped
Into your arms and threw
my glitter to the wind.

Secrets We Will Never Share

"The tongue also is a fire,"

— James 3:6.

The canine rescue shelter explains
  the cost-benefit ratio:
  puppy versus older dog
  who will have baggage.

I imagine the trauma,
  secrets Spot and I
  will never share, unlike
  my teenage roommate
  in boarding school.

One night in the dark,
  she whispered,
let's share the worst secret
that's ever happened to us.

Horrified, I listened as she spoke.
　A child asleep, she woke
　to her father licking
　her *pee pee,* like a child,
　the word
　making the incest
seem less treacherous,
more like a game, or perhaps
a way to seize the last remnant
of her stolen innocence.

Her secret burrowed
into my brain-seeking asylum,
as her father's coiled tongue
serpentined through
the inflamed arteries of our lives.

After You

Forty years after our broken
engagement, I type your name
in the search engine, reminded how
time is the monolithic
library of learning.

I could have written your bio
blind-folded:
chief of surgery
major Eastern hospital
nurse wife,
willing to re-locate
to Gotham with you, a hard
scrabble city, devoid of whimsy,
perennial sooty skies eclipsed
by steel mills, vertical cement buildings.

She was so ecstatic to be Mrs. Doctor,
grateful beyond gold – she would have
crawled into the blackest, frozen man
hole to be warmed by your halo.

You, her glittering, north Neptune,
pointing to the poshest suburb
that burg offered.

Post scriptum:
in this my last third of life,
after multiple marriages and moves,
explorations and experimentations,
I landed on the central coast, between the
sea, and the Santa Lucia mountains;
a savage landscape of volatility:
fires, mudslides, and earthquakes.
A land of hummingbirds, monarchs,
and exotic jacarandas, carpeting
my driveway in magenta splendor,
holy trumpets,
only God could have designed.

My earliest reoccurring dream
is of a wave, rolling in slow motion
up to the sky. With my last coin,
I buy a ride on it.

I am always alone,
no one to save me.
Intuiting long ago, you
my darling, God doctor
would have been wasted
on a girl like me.

Misogyny

You Bluebeards,
mesmerizing,
monstrous men.
You kings of commerce,
who capture and behead
your prize when they dare
to become real,
to use their voice,
to speak their truth,
to take action,
to use the bleeding key,
to open the forbidden doors,
to know what they know,
and see what they see.
Behind the locked door,
dead morning glories piled
blue corpses, caged in hoop skirts,
corsets, bustiers, eternally blooming
bosoms, ripe flowers waiting
for the king's kiss.
Unfathered women
with broken compasses,
destined for the dungeon.

Cleopatra

Almond emerald eyes, my black Persian
comrade in misery, flung on her pillow,
under the lace canopied bed: Her throne.
Fanned out like the choicest courtesan
of her day. Entertaining, cajoling if she found
you worthy. Her engines revved like an Italian
luxury car: major torque, rhythmic purr.
A leap into my lap, a rub between my legs.

Each fastidious, tolerating Jack the husband,
who never put the seat down, often missed.
His creations, one mess after another.
We had no use for his chaos.
Cleo looked at him imperiously.
In telepathic communion of thought, I knew
her thoughts: *grow up, baby man.*

One December morning, the cat was sick,
disoriented, helpless, her watery eyes pleading:
O God what is happening.
Jack was sleeping on his stomach. She climbed
on top, spread-eagled on his back.
Jack's stocky longshoreman body, a radiator
all winter long, became her heating pad.
She's just using me, Jack whined, his eyes opening
like a crocodile coming out of a coma.

It's not personal; cats are opportunistic.
For days, raindrop tears smeared our Brooklyn
row house windows, as winter lingered on.
Women and cats are intuitive creatures.
We both knew it was the end.

Juan & Juanita

A candlelight vigil was held to remember
those killed by domestic violence.
Violet flames danced in the dark.
Violet is the hottest fire on the color spectrum.
— *Glen Falls Gazette*

Nicknames they gave each other
for his penis, and her vagina.
The memory an eternally lit
violet vigil burning
in my young bride's heart;
I never shared such secret
intimacies with my groom.

Juanita, the invisible vagina
in our marriage. One winter night,
Juan found her on facebook. He had long
been done with me and our North country,
white-out blizzards; he was *doin time,*
waiting for that perfect *hasta luego baby* moment.

He was ready for a new vagina,
that came with sun, and a beach house
in the Hamptons.
One morning at breakfast Juan announced
he was *not happy*, and he was leaving me
for Juanita, his *"high school sweetheart,"*
in his sixties, no less.

I threw my bowl of Cheerios at him
milky white o's circled over his head,
like miniature spinning planets.
I watched my dying marriage morph
into a solar explosion,
bedazzled by a big bang ending.

O people, I wish them a lifetime
of sophomoric bliss where no
bankruptcies or betrayals ever
mar their invincibility.

"In our endings are our beginnings,"
T.S. Eliot proclaimed.

Years later, I fantasize Juan warehoused
in an existential no man's land with Alzheimer's,
no longer waxing about Juanita, *the love of his life.*
He is swimming in his own impenetrable island
a blurry horizon of sequined sea and sky.

He looks out the window,
captivated by the green flash
sinking into the sun.

Some days he will grab his torpedo-
shaped organ and shout:
 "Pow, Pow, Pow,"
thinking it is a missile.

Juanita comes to visit.
He looks past her,
bewitched by his island's
sparkling, tropical stars.
The natives call it *God's sign.*

Roaring Fork River,
Aspen Colorado

Our kismet kiss
beside the Roaring Fork,
where you held
your first rod at two,
a kiss I prepared for
since thirteen,
practicing on my pillow,
my lips sinking into feathers,
with the openness of a sky.

But nothing could have prepared
me for the surprise
of your lips somersaulting, head
over heels through endless air.

Remember that golden autumnal
afternoon, Colorado post card pretty,
miniature spinning suns twinkling,
fallen stars on the river,
the aspen forest's iridescent
leaves shimmying; schools of silver fish-tails.
Years later making love to me,
under a full wedding cake moon.

Moon Over Maine

During that summer of loosing
only the memory of the moon
      remains.
Everything else: the beach cottage,
marriage, money, children, friends
all washed away at high tide.
It was three am, the eternal orange
hour, when the explosion of moonlight
exhorted me to get up,
open the French doors
step onto the balcony, and behold:
a moon hung so low
you could almost touch it,
a neon, orange magic ball
dangling like a toy,
over Casco bay,
inviting me to play.
Presenting itself to me
as consolation, an offering
for all things disappearing;
a reminder that wonder
would never forsake me.

Ben-Wa Fun

In memory of William Butler Yeats

Two silver, shiny balls
long the secret of Chinese
women knowledgeable in the arts
of pleasure, came tumbling out of me
defiantly, like runaway gingerbread
men bouncing down the escalator,
with Christmas morning ebullience
past the commuters,
with faces vacant as pre-dawn
parking lots, on their way to
another day at the office,
without the aid
of ancient Asian arts.
My pilgrim soul in a moment
of glad grace went flying
after those toys, the size of robin's
eggs, and seizing them,
waited until the opportune moment
to place them back
inside the cloistered pink nest
for which they were designed.

In the evening, with shadows
deep, I sat in my rocker,
rolling back and forth
in front of a glowing fire
and ruminating upon those who had loved
me false, and was content to be alone
with the two who loved me true.

Counting His Lucky Stars:
Sixty-fifth Wedding Anniversary

It doesn't matter how many times
he's told the tale. Each telling
astonishes. His own bottomless
bowl of fortune cookies – good luck
filling His eyes with liquid stars.

Did I ever tell you about
How we met?
It was in the Bronx.
She was leaning against
her father's cherry red,
Oldsmobile. Cat eye sun
glasses, bouncing, pony tail,
pretty as a pinup.
I was twenty-one, and said to myself:
I am going to marry that girl;
I loved her from that first moment.

I listen stunned
by the possibility
of being imprinted
on another's heart for a lifetime.

First Kiss

Summer dance at the fair
carnival of lights flickering
like birthday cake candles,
ferris wheel mirrors spinning,
your kiss sweet as cotton candy.

Guns & Roses

What wakes me at three am
isn't the memory of hiding
to escape his knife.

It is the evening he got down
on his knees in Times Square,
and begged me for a new invention,
even though he was the sole wage earner.
It was a tender and poetic gesture
coming from a six foot man, with a wild
mane of black hair, lantern blue eyes,
and a violent streak.
Black Irish biographers wrote.

One morning after my ex
made blueberry pancakes,
he looked long at the dog
and then at me – said:
    I wish Rex could talk.
I always loved him
for that childlike wish,
with his ivy league degree,
fancy pedigrees, white house dinners –
his father dispatched by the President
to babysit for Marilyn on a bender.

Our only child tells me to *take off*
     the rose colored glasses;
get real about that narcissistic asshole.

The fiercest realty I've ever known.

Everything Changed

The night I made my prize
   chicken pot pie, perfect
   golden crust puffed up,
   like a parade float.

After orbiting nine months
  a comet around my womb,
   you exploded into the universe,
    dusky blue, wet, blood streaked.

In the cracked snapshot
  taken a lifetime ago,
  the pie plate
  hangs over my stomach
   full and round as a flying
    saucer suspended in midair.
     I looked like a carnival curiosity.
    ready to levitate.

My magnum opus,
   my heavenly poema,
      proclaiming at age five:
      "When I grow up
         I want to dust the ring around Saturn."

There was never
   another child or chicken pot pie,
      after the night everything changed.

Leaving Home

My twenty-two year old man child
stops by the house to say goodbye
before driving cross country.

I am releasing him
into America's open frontier
to find his adult wings.

I spend the day making lentil soup.
Red ham, green lentils, orange carrots,
a harvest festival of swirling autumn leaves.
Warm cheddar cheese biscuits
pillowy soft, puffed up like a parakeet,
lathered with herb butter.
These are the offerings
I bring to the alter.
Our last meal,
a layered blend of smoky, earthy, savory flavors.

As the sliver of his pick-up
fades into silver skies,
I know there will be treachery,
times he will be blindsided
by fog so thick,
the road disappears.

He learned early
the world is cruel and harsh,
laying the foundation
for resilience, coping skills,
to stay the course,
through life's vagaries.

I get down on my knees,
thankful our last supper,
a cozy concoction,
of comfort and grace.

Everything his childhood rugged geography lacked.

Last Supper

Tonight is my last supper,
not due to cancer or crucifixion,
like the good thief, I desire to join
the lover of my soul in Paradise this day.

Or perhaps I am simply weary of invisible men.
When my son was seven, he asked me,
"why is dad always hiding from us?"
Good question, but now after all these years,
the *why* that once was so paramount,
miraculously no longer exists.

Who cares what mishegas led to my ex's
disappearing acts,
he had his reasons – a thousand different moving
components
that once intrigued me. Many lives ago, he was
my king of the air:
"Why is dad always wearing his airport clothes,"
our son asked.

He flies my child.
And the truth lies more with your mom;
a poet, and guiless girl, born
with a deep penchant for enchantment.

The meal is what absorbs me most tonight.
Engagement Chicken, as it is ubiquitously known,
the dinner Megan made for Harry
on the eve of his proposal.
From the very first bite into the pillowy white
breast, adorned in a velvety, lemony, garlicy gravy,
abdication is required, to experience
its divinely dizzying effects upon the mind,
obliterating everything else, the way love does,
all except for the object of one's affections.

Allow yourself to be enveloped, my ex said
when I was a nervous, young bride,
before making love for the first time.

Tonight, the Holy Ghost will come upon me
in a celestial overshadowing, filling me,
with divinity, and I will become
His Mystical Goddess.

> **Mishegas**: a Yiddish word, meaning craziness;
> encompassing all that is fucked up.
> — *Urban Dictionary*

When You Introduce Me

To your wife, I will walk
on egg shells, fragile things,
easily cracked, like a newborn,
reminding me of all my fears
as a young, unmothered woman,
holding the soft orb
of your wobbly head,
in my cupped hands,
as if in prayer,
always so afraid of breaking you,
nothing so small and alive
in all the world,
as your minuscule, mottled arms,
swimming minnows through the air.

No need to worry that I will be
any of the mother-in-law stereotypes.
You will never have to choose.
I have prepared for this visit
your whole life, when I will bow
to your bride and become
the invisibly beloved.

Wedding Dress

You need something special
something that bespeaks,
mother of the groom,
sales lady pitch.

And there it was—
hanging on a wall
in a corner, almost invisible,
as I must become,
a woman in the background.

You know the old adage:
"A son is a son until he takes a wife,
a daughter is a daughter all her life."
I raised him for this moment
to adore his queen,
knowing I would become her subject;
the sacrificial lamb in her kingdom.

A mother makes sacrifices
for the man child she birthed
thirty-five years ago,
weighing twelve pounds,
when I was only a wisp,
wrists slender as a swan's neck.

The birth blew me apart
like a city under siege,
cutting off my breath,
strangling me in waves
until I went into shock,
eyes rolling back in my head,
like cherries spinning
in a Vegas slot machine.

Everyone said I would forget
that joy would replace
the memory of being murdered.

"The Happiest Place on Earth"
Disney billboard slogan

Florida, land of sleaze, hurricanes,
and those sci-fi, cartoon, palmetto bugs –
in truth, prettied up cockroaches –
infesting the artificially landscaped swamp.

Florida, the place where a boy
who wore Spider-Man boots,
still believed in magic, built ornate
sand castles along the shore's edge,
complete with torture and death towers,
to battle ever-lurking villains.

Then one day, like some macabre scene
out of a horror movie, life imitated art,
as a seven foot, primeval reptile rose
out of the water, mouth opened wide
as the world, and swallowed that boy,
in the black dungeon of its armored belly.

Crazy things happen in this savage
world, where Blackbeard runs around,
chopping off everyone's heads.
We die as we live. This super hero's death was valiant;
beyond what he might have ever imagined.

Gift From U.S. Poet Laureate

His letter is so elegant.
I picture him
as Cary Grant wearing a silk cravat,
draped over a chaise, self-amused,
blowing smoke rings that sway
through the air like hula hips.
He glides through his domain
pirouetting as he sips
a glass of aged Dom,
handing his fluted Baccarat
to the invisible, yet omniscient
English Butler.
It is time to get down to business,
a secretary to the morning.

My darling, he reassures me
with the wand of his Montblanc,
tend to your own roses. All those
cavemen, sitting around a fire,
they don't know how to light
have nothing to offer.

Rilke's spirit blazes through
the opaque paper. *There is only
one thing you should do.
Go into yourself. Excavate.*

Stunned by his generosity
I marvel at the blessing bestowed,
a miniature sterling silver hoe.

Poetry Workshop

Our renowned poetess, teacher
asks us to read our favorite poem.
When You Are Old, by Yeats.
I am composed until I get to the line –
But one man loved the pilgrim soul in you.

Tears flow, too many to catch,
words blur,
I am unable to read the poem,
a tidal wave of lament, stemming
from my ancestral women's tribe,
wailing in the wasteland
cries from un-fathered women
cursed in choosing men
with no eyes to see or mirror,
their moments of glad grace,
or the beauty, and sorrows
of their changing faces.

Ghostly fathers, husbands,
brothers, and sons restlessly pace,
upon the mountains, their heads
hidden in a sea of stars.

Lockdown

Pasha: royal, noble, honored one, most
powerful lord.
- Persian translation

In these dog days of pandemic
all the clocks have stopped.

One day slips seamlessly
into the next,
without name.
Saturday, Sunday, Monday,
all the same.

The dog's day doesn't change.
He is doin' time.
Wake-up, eat, play, poop,
sleep, walk, do it all again,
and again, ad infinitum,
endlessly digging to China.

His instinct is for routine.
Mine is for change.

Maybe today he will talk,
console me with life's hidden meaning,
that only he has doggie access to.

Bless me with a prophetic message.
Be stouthearted and wait.

My little pasha robed in ermine,
crowned with divine patience.

What do you wait for?

During these dog days,
show me how
to be curled in contentment,
as these black days
tunnel on and on.

Pie in Pandemic

Yesterday, I refused to be quarantined
for one more minute.
Dog was antsy too,
turning in endless circles,
unable to find a place to curl.
I packed us up in the car, a mental health
emergency day, and drove that fairytale,
glitter of sea from Morro Bay to Cambria.

I bought a piece of luscious homemade
rhubarb, raspberry pie warmed,
vanilla bean ice cream on top.
Pie will always be an essential service,
a necessary balm,
sweetening life's brutalities.

Pie makes us simultaneously grateful
and forgetful, transporting us back
to a front porch with rockers,
magical time without worries,
enabling us to savor the sublime,
a timeless river of sweet and tart.

On a sad Sunday during pandemic,
I ate pie along Moonstone road
that runs parallel to the Pacific.
I pulled over on a stretch of sand
watching waves break and curl,
rugged cliffs hugging the cove,
the Hearst castle rising
out of the clouds
like an apparition.

Immersed in storybook enchantment,
I ponder my karmic fortune.

Paschal Pink Moon

Named after a pink wildflower blooming in early spring.
— *Old Farmer's Almanac*

Tonight, let us awaken
to the magnanimous pink moon,
the way she follows you,
like a besotted suitor,
no matter where you turn,
lit up like a crystal chandelier,
hanging from heaven.

Remember Easter in all her pink,
purple, and yellow pastels, gay
as a debutante, not even pandemic
can stop her pink blazing blooms,
from falling between the cracks
of our curtained world.

Levity In Lock-down

Pandemic 2020

Jax is not in lock-down.
In truth, he is having a ball,
as evidenced by the pictures,
and report card sent from
his first day at doggy pet resort,
for reasons known to God alone,
considered an essential service.

Reported are his doggy friend favs,
top of the list is chi chi
woo woo a bossy black pug,
who runs the show, a fun fireball,
gets everybody jazzed,
for a dip in the pool, a game of chase.

There is a picture of them
standing on hunches hugging.
Jax looks blissed-out.
Chi chi has that effect on males,
the owner reports.
She's a love goddess.

High Tops

You never saw the boys in daylight
just hundreds of their high top sneakers
tied over Brooklyn telephone pole wires,
as if in some exotic tribal code, that cried
out to the world: I exist.
I own this crib.

I couldn't fully comprehend at twenty-five
with my day job in Manhattan and dreamy
future, burning like birthday cake candles
across the sky,
living in the projects,
was not a way station for them.

The invisible boys could remove
a television from your car in the time
it took you to climb the stoop to your
brownstone studio and unlock the door.
They knew when your back was turned,
through camouflaged jungle eyes,
they watched everything you did.

Hot summer nights
you could hear their deep guttural
voices crashing, tires screeching,
head on collisions, followed by gun shots.

Sunday mornings the streets filled
with the holy silence of a graveyard.
I walked to the corner bodega,
picked up the Times.

"Hey, Laura Ashley," the man behind the counter
said every week. *"You back again?"*
He half expected this would be the day
when the silver, spidery bridge, splattered
with its defiant graffiti, the color of a badly beaten
prize fighter, would carry me over to the new
life that awaited me, across the river on an island,
where a shrine of clustered skyscrapers glittered
in the distance like jewel encrusted crowns.

Divine Assignment in Brooklyn

Pajamas my uniform, I send up prayer
petitions for a living, neon pink lighted flares,
wiggly smoke caterpillars blazing heavenward.

Our longings have a short life
id driven, fickle things, dazzling
as the metallic Blue Morpho's wings;
shimmering wildly, with parallelizing
beauty, ignorant of death,
to follow their orgasmic bliss.

I dwell in a railroad flat, in Red Hook
on the threshold of migraine; a world
of spinning rooms and flashing stars beacon.

Cries for Eden fly over
an indifferent urbanscape:
bodegas, black-tarred roofs,
fire escapes and sidewalk stoops,
where neighbors sit in folding chairs,
behind chain-link wire, watching.

Mary, the welfare mother
five children, with different men,
sells her sweet potato pies, warm
cinnamon clouds, float above,
the little chapel on the corner;
projects behind it, basketballs
pound their daily ghetto drum beat.

Curry perfumes the Sunday air.
Across the spidery Brooklyn Bridge,
Gotham, glows like the Hope Diamond.
I walk back and forth across the bridge,
staring at the gleaming silver vertical
buildings brushing the sky
dreaming of a way out.

Mary's Poetic Sweet Potato Pie

Thirty-five years
since I last saw you,
a single, welfare mother,
five boys with different men,
sitting on your stoop in Brooklyn,
across from mine.

Our neighborhood becoming gentrified
with folks like me in their thirties,
commuting to Wall Street,
shopping at the corner bodega,
the sound of hoops, hard bouncing
balls, against sizzling summer pavement,
the scent of curry rising on Sundays,
from the housing projects behind our street.

I was simply passing through
imagining palm trees, winter sun,
someday never having to shovel
sooty snowy flakes piled on top
of each other like heavy wet blankets.

Your *poetic pies* transformed all
the black and red graffiti, dripping
vampire blood covering the hood,
into a bite of euphoric sweet, a melding
delight of cinnamon, and savory ginger,
lifting my sagging spirits out of the ghetto blues.

How to Know if a Poem is Any Good

Wendell Berry said, if you have to ask,
better to stop writing, because you'll never know.
But I know.
I know the poem, is good when it morphs
into a magic carpet,
flying me through many incarnations,
surprising me with its freshness years later,
when it still tastes good and fresh,
like warm gingerbread, just out of the oven.
It is good company, I don't feel
so alone in its presence, it reminds me
there is a world beyond, the asphalt
and cement where fireflies turn
into orange, neon stars, and trees talk,
making this mundane earth more magical

Peaches

Glistening on a south Florida fruit stand
translucent skin, soft and fuzzy,
like a prepubescent boy's face, kissable
ripe, juicy, ready to implode.
A bite of angel food.
Everything you could want in life
      is in a peach.

Dentist's Chair

He drills deliriously away,
face half hidden behind mask
black rodent eyes, zooming in
on targeted tooth with intensity
of a cat capturing its prey.
He is happily animated
working inside the mouth,
his unique domain.
His high pitched drill screeches
like a trapped mouse.

Sting's melodious voice, sings
through my headphones:
Feel her body rise
when you kiss her mouth
among the fields of gold.

The nitrous has kicked in.
Behind my shut eyes
I see the wheat colored sun,
sinking in the sky,
children running home.

I'm lost in deep golden
fields that go on forever.
Surprised not even the drugs
have obliterated the wanting
to be found.

Missing the Signs

How is it possible
to drive on a California freeway
in the wrong direction,
oblivious to collision,
going through a red light,
racking up three tickets in a week.

The therapist speaks: *You are in shock*
operating in a fog – admonishes me,
for driving in suicidal state.

How could I have not seen:
The red light
The on-ramp sign: wrong direction
The man I love
turning on me;
a rabid Rottweiler,
jumping for my jugular,
manically shaking me
in its jaws,
until my back breaks.

She is a therapist familiar,
with the nuances of treachery.
You never see betrayal coming,
that's why it is shocking.

Shock: the first grief step.
Definition: a cruel catastrophe
leaving you unmercifully mangled,
without the grace to kill you.

Remembering:
Holocaust Museum in Washington, D.C.

I read how real it was, designed for a visitor
to relive the experience of a prisoner.

Given a number, herded into a sterile
elevator overflowing with people,
all of us squeezed in together,
dumb, helpless cattle. Our eyes, glassy,
and dazed, like uncomprehending animals.

O God, we pled to the invisible wizard
in the sky, whose arms we prayed would drop
down like bull rope, and lift us up from this dung
heap,
as if only faith in pure goodness,
could render such virulent, evil bearable.

We don't yet know of the ovens waiting to turn us
into ash, or the dark mercy that will come in death.

My visit took place forty years ago.
I still remember when I became unglued,
when it became too real.
I had to be escorted to the museum's
waiting room, to recover my composure.

It was the shoes.
Seeing an entire room filled,
floor to ceiling
with prisoner's shoes. I saw them,
piled on top of one another;
a heap of slaughtered ghosts,
mothers, fathers, and children,
who once wore Mary Janes,
picnicking together in edelweiss meadows,
wreathed with lilies around Bavarian lakes.

Tears spewed out of me, like a busted fire
hydrant. The ax of man's monstrous cruelty,
hacking away at the frozen sea within,
the slaughter of holy innocents,
their hundreds of thousands of empty shoes,
searing the massacre in my heart forever.

An older woman sat down next to me.
She said, *You are not Jewish.*
My blonde hair and blue eyes betraying me.
We built this museum for people like you,
to never forget, to never stop crying.

Peony Parade

Parading through peony petticoats,
their dizzying lushness a cabaret
of ruffled skirts kicked up in a French
can-can. Hundreds of varieties,
displayed in the gardens, with names
conjuring romance, sex and theater:
Gay Paree, Bride's Dream, Pillow Talk,
Angel's Cheeks – extravagant show offs,
screaming: *look at me, look at me –*
cartwheeling children, bursting
with their own magnificence.
Breathless, I bury my head in a honeyed
cluster of Sarah Bernhardts.
The grower tells me she is a classic,
winner of the American Peony Society
gold medal – a study in contrasts,
at once wild, and ruthlessly demure;
beloved bride of my heart.

The Surprise of Solace

Angelonia 'Angelface Blue' (Summer Snapdragon),
is a tender perennial with deep violet-blue showy
blooms.
— *Garden Handbook*

On an ordinary Monday,
the soothing sound of a machine
buzzes across the field,
lazy summer bees burrow
into angelface blue snapdragons
their bellies swollen with nectar,
happily reminding me:
someone is doing their job
someone has a schedule
someone is being productive
someone is being paid.
This is the American way.

My vocation is to stand
    on the edges
observe, listen, and record,
    to be surprised.
    An unpaid poet,
ready to catch sapphires,
falling out of the blue.
    My remuneration
a price beyond pearls:
communion with the divine.

Picasso in Black Hoodie

Painters Are Failed Poets,
— Neruda

He enters at the end
of my dream, slips in
through the fire escape
   gangster style.
The master misogynist,
with deep black coffee
bean bulging bull eyes,
pans the entire room
with their wide angle lens,
sits on my bed, whispers,
Find your gift and then give it away.
We are all with you.
Death has blessed the black angel
with a generous spirit. He joins
a cloud of witnesses lifting me up,
in a poetic candlelit vigil,
his close friend, the other Pablo,
fixates on the flickering flames,
imagines shimming hipped hula girls
dancing barefoot on heaven's dome,
   breathing in God.

Flurries Falling on Lake Isabelle

All night white sequins fall
tu tu's pirouetting through winter skies,
in the morning frozen
swans on a lake of tears.

Wheels & Wings

Today I will wash my car
gifting me with peace,
angelic as pearls,
vacuum crumbs on carpet,
sundry strewn scraps,
blow up all the fragments,
into a winged cherub
of opalescent order.

Ambien Ache

responds to my wailing lament,
shrill as a sea gull, in a solo sky.
Tiny pink pill bestows visions:
wreathed flower girls, vestal virgins,
eternal ingénues, carefree dancing
debutantes, waltzing in white chiffon.

Voices beckon me to swallow
the poppies, lie down in petals
polished as pink pearls, forget
the bogeyman disguised
as a prince, trolling the ballroom,
dangling sweet dreams.

> **Vestal Virgins:** Priestesses consecrated to the
> Roman goddess Vesta and to the service of watching
> the sacred fire perpetually kept burning on her altar.
> — *Merriam-Webster Dictionary*

Workshop On Aging

The gerontologist said,
you don't know anything
before the age of sixty.
A psychologist piped up,
I would say seventy.
Picasso said: *It takes a long time*
to grow young.

My wish is live like a child,
or a dog in the vast unknown,
under an erased, chalk board sky,
wordless and white as a bride,
implanted with the divine seed
of knowing only how to love
and be loved, before the world
graffiti-smeared your pink heart,
raw as a sand crab without its shell.

It takes an eternity to reclaim yourself.

Solar Eclipse

Oregon was crazed; Y2K all over again,
warnings of computers shutting down
highways blocked, grocery store shelves
bare; a war zone.

Catastrophizing about the eclipse
created diversion –
the Korean lunatic's threats,
Isis' latest decapitations,
an eclipse could not mutilate,
only blind us,
only if we looked directly at it.

Crescent shadows flowing,
a galaxy of black capes
flung over the world,
transforming day into night. En masse,
in special solar glasses,
we looked up,
divining an omen.

Solar Eclipse, 2017
(Touch down 10:15am, Oregon)

Shock

Doesn't it sound like a futuristic
shocking *Brave New World* sometime
    in the far away.

Last week the pink barn
was bulldozed; the funky,
quirky soul of our town,
standing in the middle of a field,
surrounded by tall grasses & wild
flowers, spreading out as far
as the endless blue.
Call it a sense of forever.

Chain stores in a neutered mall
will replace the barn and fields,
a reminder of all that you lack.
The pink barn offered
itself to your imagination;
with gifts of whimsy & wonder,
filling the ache of wanting more.

Good night giggle moon
who made the poetic pink barn
twinkle in the starry darkness,
making my heart somersault,
    like a first kiss,
each time I drove by.

Redemption

Born to bloom
a wild violet, resilient
unconquerable spirit,
buried under snow,
steely blue, purple petals peek
through intermittent winter sun.

Crushed upon the heels of men
violets baby breath blossoms,
perfume the air in forgiveness.

Saint Francis' Feast Day

My pup is five months old
in the shy stage,
according to behavioral experts.
He sticks close, some body part
always touching, at night curling
inside my hollowed half-moon.

At daily mass, he lays by my hip
skin to skin, contentedly gnawing
on a bone, the way some women
rhythmically knit, absorbed
in secret worlds.
The priest admonishes us,
be obsessed with God. As if on cue,
pup drops his beloved bone, leaps
from the pew, God possessed,
in a flash of flying fur races up
up to the alter, as if spotting
another dog, a bacon treat, some
crazy lure compelling him
into a deep, impenetrable trance.
The priest did not miss a beat,
masterfully weaving in the next
surprise stitch:
this pup is obsessed with God,
Saint Francis would be pleased.

Poppy Love

You pay more for this rare color, the breeder said.
He is more precious than rubies,
and nothing you desire can compare to him.

Puppy breath…O the smell of you:
    circus and zoo,
a sugary blend of cotton candy,
crushed peanuts, and popcorn.

Costumed in Halloween orange fur –
imagine wild, winter poppies
waltzing on California's coastal hillsides.

You, the big surprise
in this second half of life,
my cinnamon fur-child.

Trapeze artist flying
    through the air,
landing in my lap,
    lathers my face,
with whipped, feathery, angel kisses.

Getting ready for bed,
hidden chew toys and treats
fall out of my bra,
bones buried in the crack
of my couch, at night,
your furry neck, curled
in my nape.

Coffee in the morning
you snuggle next to me,
chewing on buffalo bone.
Sunlight beams through
the kitchen window, encircling us
in a honeyed-moon halo.

Someday my sweet potato pie,
you will tell me your hopes,
as you have listened
so intently to all of mine,
as if my hopes,
were the most important thing
in the world.
Your head-cocked
in a heart-breaking attempt,
to understand life's imponderables.

Ode to Child Poet

Every morning on my walk
to third grade,
Mrs. Pangburn's prize
 winning hydrangea.
 beckoned me like a promethean,
periwinkle snow cone, blazing
at a state fair,
under a merciless desert sun,
dripping glistening icy lushness,
to come and lick it
or perhaps pick it,
and risk Mrs. Pangburn's violent
one eyed, cyclopitic vengeance.
All that protected her voluptuous blooms
was her legendary temper,
and my childish fears:
she feasted on the flesh
of little girls and dipped
their pony tails in cat pee,
dooming them to an eternally
ammonia stench embalmment,
ensuring the prince's kiss,
would never touch their frozen lips.

After forty years,
I still remember the deep ache
for that incandescent splendor,
a prepubescent hunger
for transcendent beauty.

Ether

The memory of childhood
shiny black balloon
lowered over your face,
the sickeningly sweet smell
of cheap perfume,
reminiscent of the witch's cloying
breath as she lures you into her lair,
prepares to cut your tonsils out.

You fall into a deep sleep.
She scissors snip, snip, snip.

Wake-up to cherry popsicles
trickling down your raw throat.

Muse

Headed south on 101 toward Santa Barbara.
The Pacific stretches out like a sequined starfish.
Santa Ynez mountains ring around
a horse shoe framing the glittering sea.

Jim Morrison sings Light My Fire.
Radio blasting through mecca;
the Monte Carlo of America.
Shiny buttercup suns spread across the sky,
speckling the mountains with pink
and gold sparkles.

Morrison pulls you deep into the music,
like you are on a stoned out binge, right along
with him.
Soma in the air, brain deadening
earthquake manic energy
simmering beneath the surface.
So many California blonde
vacant sunflower faces.

Camille was ten last time she was on this highway.
It was raining with smoky fog hovering
beneath the clouds.
The mountains look sad today, Mom.
They look like they're crying."
I knew she would be unfit for anything
in the world
a stranger in a strange land, with a pilgrim soul,
who became Morrison's muse.

Empress of Wonder

Bessie Smith was known as:
"The Empress of Blues."
She sang, *Nobody knows you*
when you're down and out.
I would like my epithet to be:
The Empress of Wonder.
One who seeds stars in the gutter.

Gravestone Epitaph

Poet
Pilgrim soul
Prophet
Mystic
Wounded healer
Truth teller
Seeker and learner
Bearer of light
One who lived hidden
embraced in God's womb,
of holy wonder and love.
Empress of Wonder.

O My Darling

You choose to become a doctor or a lawyer,
but one is chosen for the sacred art of poetry.
— Lord Byron

Today I look at the only picture
to survive the rubble
of your childhood,
where no birthdays
were celebrated, or hands held.
Your stringy unbrushed hair
hangs like brittle winter twigs.

When a little money came my way
I bought a vintage, heart-shaped frame;
a valentine for God's poema,
the one who triumphed
over violence, combat and betrayal.

Forty years later,
your framed face
looks back at me,
a shell-shocked, immigrant,
child's face, that has witnessed
unspeakable horrors.

You are four years old
in the faded, black-and-white,
tattered photograph. One scrap
of evidence found in the ruins;
a testament that you were not
rendered completely invisible.

Today I honor your rugged journey,
hold your orphaned hand,
       in my hand.

Today tangerine trees sparkle
like miniature California suns,
bougainvillea blooms madly, carpeting
our garden with magenta-petaled jewels;
favorite childhood crayon color.

Today I am reminded of *fioretti,*
little flowers God sends to delight us
      along the tortuous way.

Expressions of Gratitude

EXPRESSIONS OF GRATITUDE TO
the following places, and poets who provided
encouragement and support along my poetic path.

Sarah Lawrence
Boston University
Breadloaf Writer's Conference
Wesleyan Writer's Conference

Thomas Lux, Edward Brathwaite,
Derik Walcott, Linda Pastan,
Nancy Willard, Sue Ellen Thompson,
Perrie Longo, Elena Karina Byrne,
and Ann Dernier.

A special thanks to my angels of inner hospitality,
Adele Zelena & Karla Martinez

A special thank-you to Benjamin Daniel Lawless
for his vision & expertise in bringing my first
collection of poetry to fruition.

Grateful acknowledgment to Kamil Vojnar for his
cover photograph, *Angel Dreams*.

Made in the USA
Coppell, TX
07 June 2020